W9-ATE-521

OCT 1988
RECEIVED
OHIO DOMINICAN
COLLEGE LIBRARY
COLUMBUS, OHIO
43219

PUBLIC LIBRARY
DISCARD
COLUMBUS, OHIO

LUMBUS COMMUNITY BIBLE COLLEGE
COLUMBUS, OHIO

There are perhaps a hundred thousand species or kinds of butterflies.

"Possibly no other living creature in our natural world catches our eye quite so immediately as the butterfly."

TROPICAL BUTTERFLIES

By ALEXANDER B. KLOTS
Research Associate, Department of Insects and Spiders
The American Museum of Natural History, New York

Illustrations by Robert Borja

CHILDRENS PRESS, Chicago

Original copyright © 1960, Columbia Record Club, Inc.,New York, N.Y.,under the title of
Tropical Butterflies (Colorslide Nature and Science Program). All rights reserved. New edition
published 1968 by Regensteiner Publishing Enterprises, Inc., Chicago. Published
simultaneously in Canada. Lithographed in the U.S.A.
Library of Congress Catalog Number: 68-14724.

PICTURE ACKNOWLEDGMENTS

The color photographs in *Tropical Butterflies* are the work of the following photographers
and artists, whose collaboration is gratefully acknowledged. For the color photographs,
Alexander B. Klots (pages 24, 25, 26, 27, 28, 34, 38, 39, 40, 42, 47, 51, 55, 56, 58); Dr. Edward S.
Ross (pages 32, 33, 35, 36, 37, 41, 43, 44, 45, 46, 48, 49, 50, 52, 53, 57); CCM: General
Biological Inc., Chicago (pages 8, 11, 12, 13, 14, 15, 17, 19, 21, 29). For the black-and-white
photographs we wish to thank Dr. Edward S. Ross (pages 10, 18). Illustration on page 23
by Margrit Fiddle. Front matter illustrations by Robert Borja.

J
595.78
K

CONTENTS

69-065076

BKM
53

127413

TROPICAL BUTTERFLIES

POSSIBLY NO OTHER LIVING CREATURE IN OUR NATURAL WORLD catches our eye quite so immediately as the butterfly.

We suddenly see a flicker of wings across the forest floor and catch a glimpse of dazzling color. Perhaps a sunbeam spotlights an explorer butterfly perched motionless on a flower, beautifully dramatic. Or, as thousands of butterflies cluster around a shallow pool to drink, they form a matchless blanket of beauty.

Butterflies without knowing it have been the reason for great human conflicts. In medieval days, ancient records tell how a fall of "red rain" started a wave of terror that spread across whole countrysides, often ending in fear-driven bloody fights. Today we know that this "red rain" was made by thousands of butterflies. When passing overhead, each butterfly released a drop of red liquid, causing the red rain.

his is a natural phenomenon of butterflies who have just ʃt their cocoons and begun their adult life. However, medieval people did not know this. They thought it was a supernatural action and reacted violently. So it is that the unknowing butterfly has had his day in the making of human history.

Courtesy of CCM: General Biological Inc., Chicago

Butterflies are of the order Lepidoptera (from the Greek *lepis*, scale, and *pteron*, wing). Lepidoptera is pronounced *lep-ih*-DOPP-*ter-ah*. A lepidopterist is "one who studies butterflies." There are perhaps a hundred thousand species or kinds of butterflies. They are second in number only to the order of beetles and weevils, which is called Coleoptera. More people are interested in butterflies and moths than in any other order of insects. The collection and study of the many specimens can lead to distant and adventurous places, for the Lepidoptera may be found in every part of the world where there are insects, except Antarctica.

Probably the most fascinating thing of all is the way in which a member of this order develops. It begins life as a *larva*, which we call a "caterpillar." Then it enters another stage as a *pupa*, which we know as a "cocoon." The pupa, spun by the larva or caterpillar, is its protective chamber. When it finally leaves the pupa, the larva is an entirely different creature. It has become the beautiful, winged, eye-catching butterfly or moth. This process of development — from larva to pupa to adult form — is known as *metamorphosis*.

Watching this changeover process never ceases to amaze scientists and laymen alike. We will see the metamorphosis of a Monarch butterfly. As we watch the different steps and learn about various species of butterflies, we shall gain a greater appreciation for the wonders found in nature.

Courtesy of CCM: General Biological Inc., Chicago

CATERPILLARS ARE IMPORTANT

Most of our book is devoted to the last stage of the Lepidoptera, showing the beautiful adult butterflies. But first, we must discuss some of the ways in which the larvae (caterpillars) are important to man. A caterpillar's life is devoted to eating, digesting, and storing as much food as possible. Some kinds of larvae even enter homes looking for food. Some caterpillars eat clothes, or furs, as well as food. Others are plant-eaters, which attack and eat crops. These plant-eating caterpillars have frequently been put to good use. Early in the 1900's, sixty million acres of valuable Australian grazing and wheat land were taken over by the prickly pear cacti. This cacti took so much food from the soil that they killed off the less sturdy grasses. Before long, acres of valuable land were completely overgrown with this impossible thorny growth. Nothing could stop this destruction until a small moth (the cactus moth, *Cactoblastis cactorum*) was brought to Australia from Argentina and was turned loose on the cacti. The larvae of this moth dug tunnels in the pulpy stems of the prickly pear cacti. Through these tunnels, disease organisms entered and before long killed most of the cacti. The little cactus moth saved the day for the Australians. Today millions of acres, once overgrown with cacti, are now fertile enough for growing crops and grazing sheep.

Courtesy of CCM: General Biological Inc., Chicago

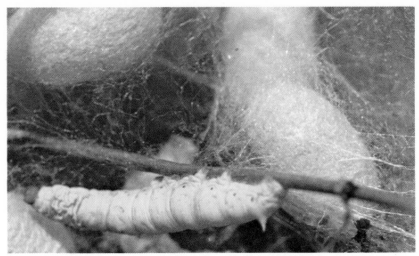

Courtesy of CCM: General Biological Inc., Chicago

Another moth which has been helpful to mankind is the silkworm. We do not think of silk as the product of a moth in the larval stage, but that is just what it is. The lives of most silkworm caterpillars, at least when they are small, are centered on a thread of silk. That thread is continually spun with every movement. The silk comes from openings near the moth's mouth called spinnerets. The silk from the spinnerets is made up of two liquids which harden as they hit the air.

The caterpillar uses the silk thread as a pathway, always spinning it from its front end, continuously coating the surface on which it is crawling. Its feet cling to this coating so that it is able to hold fast. It can move along on anything, no matter how slippery. If the caterpillar should happen to fall or drop, the spinneret continues to spin out the silken thread, and the caterpillar swings from it in midair. In this way, it can escape non-flying insect enemies which it might meet.

The silkworm *(Bombyx mori)* is simply a tamed caterpillar with a great capacity for producing silk thread. This silk is later woven into fabric. Sometimes one-fourth of the body weight in an adult silkworm is given over to the silk-producing glands. As we have noted, the silk thread, coming from the spinneret, is made by two liquids. When it hardens in the air, one forms a cover around the other. Sometimes there is a special coloring matter in this thread. This color comes from pigment in the caterpillar's food. Thus, silkworms can spin yellow silk or brown silk. Others spin a silk that glitters.

13

SENSE OF TASTE AND TOUCH

Adult butterflies have many interesting and unique body characteristics. For instance, the butterfly has a tubular proboscis, often called the tongue. This tonguelike part sucks liquids into the mouth. Normally this organ is carried coiled up below the butterfly's head like a watch spring. When stimulated, the tongue is straightened out and thrust deep into some flower or other source of liquid food. This stimulation comes from the butterfly's sense of taste. The chief sense of taste that causes the uncoiling of the tongue before feeding begins, surprisingly enough, is not found in the head at all. It is found on the soles of the butterfly's feet! When a moth or butterfly lands on a flower, the sweet, sticky surface of the flower is tasted first by the feet. These organs automatically touch off a reflex mechanism that unrolls the tongue or tubular proboscis.

One type of butterfly, the Monarch, has been carefully studied. Scientists have done experiments that demonstrate how sensitive these taste organs are. The results show that Monarch butterflies will react even if a solution has only 1/120,000,000 part of sugar to one part of water. This butterfly's sensitivity of taste is 2,408 times as great as that of the human tongue.

Courtesy of CCM: General Biological Inc., Chicago

COLORS OFFER PROTECTION

Another characteristic of the butterfly is one we are most familiar with — the bright coloration of its wings. Sir Winston Churchill once bought from a dealer a number of living butterflies, and then released them to decorate a garden party, a charming gesture of appreciation for this wonder of nature. But there is more to the butterfly than just beautiful colors and fantastic patterns on the wing. The bright colors and bold patterns in many butterflies are a warning. They tell butterfly hunters such as birds or monkeys that they are "distasteful" and would not be good to eat. Perhaps they also warn their enemies that if attacked they will spray them with an unpleasant odor. One group (the Heliconiids), for example, is particularly noted for its bitter odor, which is noticeable to humans as much as ten yards away. The bright colors of the butterflies are really the opposite of man's advertising — they warn others not to sample the product!

Courtesy of CCM: General Biological Inc., Chicago

There are many other ways butterflies and moths use color to protect themselves from injury or death. A number of insects are very dangerous to other animals. Some butterflies pretend to be these other insects. They have developed markings on their bodies or wings which look like those of insects which are "distasteful." Thus, although they themselves are not bad to eat, they share in the protection nature has given those creatures who are. An example of this method of protection or mimicry is a group of Syntomid moths. These moths have small, transparent wings and other features or characteristics that mimic wasps. The *Sesia apiformis* has clear wings, yellow-and-black body markings, and is good at looking like and pretending to be a hornet.

Many butterflies and moths have curiously different underwing and over wing patterns and colors. One great class of moths (*Catocala*), for instance, is extremely difficult to see when it is resting on a tree trunk. This moth's front wings are a very soft color with a barklike pattern. When they are folded back, they completely cover the moth's body and hind wings. The hind wings, however, are usually brilliantly colored with bold black bands and spots on a yellow, scarlet, orange, or red background. When these wings are open in flight, the moths are as easily seen as they were hard to see when only the barklike front wings showed. This is called "flash coloration," and is used by moths and butterflies to confuse attackers. It works in two ways. The moth resting on a tree may be suddenly surprised by a bird, in spite of its attempt to camouflage itself by matching the color and pattern of bark. When the moth takes to flight, the brilliant flash of color of its hind wings may surprise the bird for a minute and give the moth the time needed for a head start or escape. On the other hand, when the moth is in flight and its attacker swoops in, the attacker's attention is normally fixed on the moth's most outstanding part, its bright hind wings. When the moth dodges around a tree trunk, it quickly plasters itself flat against the bark, completely covering its bright hind wings with its barklike front ones. It now looks so much like the bark, that the hunter may fly right past, looking all around for the bright colored meal it was following.

16

Courtesy of CCM: General Biological Inc., Chicago

COLLECTING BUTTERFLIES

There are endless other interesting facts about the Lepidoptera (butterflies) which lead one deeper and deeper into this scientific study, too much to be contained in a single book. But before we begin to look at some of the beautiful members of this order we must discuss the ways in which we can increase our enjoyment and appreciation.

First we should consider the pleasures of collecting butterflies.

Almost everybody loves to collect things. You can collect stamps, seashells, ornamental buttons, or even old automobiles and have a lot of fun doing it. No matter what you collect, you develop a deeper knowledge of your subject, increase your interest in the world around you, broaden your personal experience, and make new friends through swapping items from your collection and exchanging information.

Butterflies are fun at home, too. Two intent young students observe the rearing of the Papilio philenor butterfly.

Butterfly collecting does all these things for you, and more. It brings you out into the open and introduces you to a number of different environments or surroundings. If you are able to travel with your hobby, it will take you into new geographic areas, giving you the opportunity to meet people from all over the world. If you cannot add to your collection by going outside yourself, you can still collect butterflies. You can buy your butterflies at special stores. Then mount, identify, and classify your samples. Butterflies are small enough so that a good collection may be kept in a rather small space.

18

Courtesy of CCM: General Biological Inc., Chicago

Far and above all of these reasons for collecting butterflies is the very personal reward that every collector gains. The rows of neatly spread butterflies, some brilliantly colored, others more exquisitely and delicately patterned, are equal to a trayful of precious jewels. Their beauty is such that it can be enjoyed over and over again. And the time will come to the collector when each one will be treasured less for itself than for the memories it may recall. Colin Wyatt, English traveler, writer, and butterfly collector, once wrote:

> *"I enjoy looking through my collection for the sheer beauty of the butterflies alone, but greatest, I think, is the pleasure one gets on a dull winter's day, recalling some sunny spot in a far-off land, the warmth of the air, the scents of the flowers, adventures with strange peoples, and all the incidents of the day a particular specimen was caught."
>
> "In this light, a collection becomes a thing alive, stirring the chords of memory as few other things do."

NEEDED EQUIPMENT

The collector must realize that his butterflies are very, very delicate. Their value is greatly damaged if the tiny scales which cover the wings and the body are rubbed off, or if fragile antennae or legs are broken. For this reason, the collector must use great care in handling his butterflies.

Certain basic equipment is needed and much of it can be made at home. You need a net, killing bottles, a pair of forceps, paper triangles or envelopes, and a storage jar or box. When you work on your collection at home, you need insect pins, pinning forceps, spreading boards, glass strips, a relaxing box, black India ink, paper for labels, scissors, and boxes for storing specimens. The bibliography at the end of this book lists books that have more information on how to make or obtain the things you will need as a collector, on methods of collecting specimens, finding and rearing larvae, and other subjects of interest to the serious lepidopterist.

*Wyatt, Colin. *Going Wild*. London: Hollis and Carter, 1955.

Courtesy of CCM: General Biological Inc., Chicago

BUTTERFLIES AND MOTHS
ORDER LEPIDOPTERA

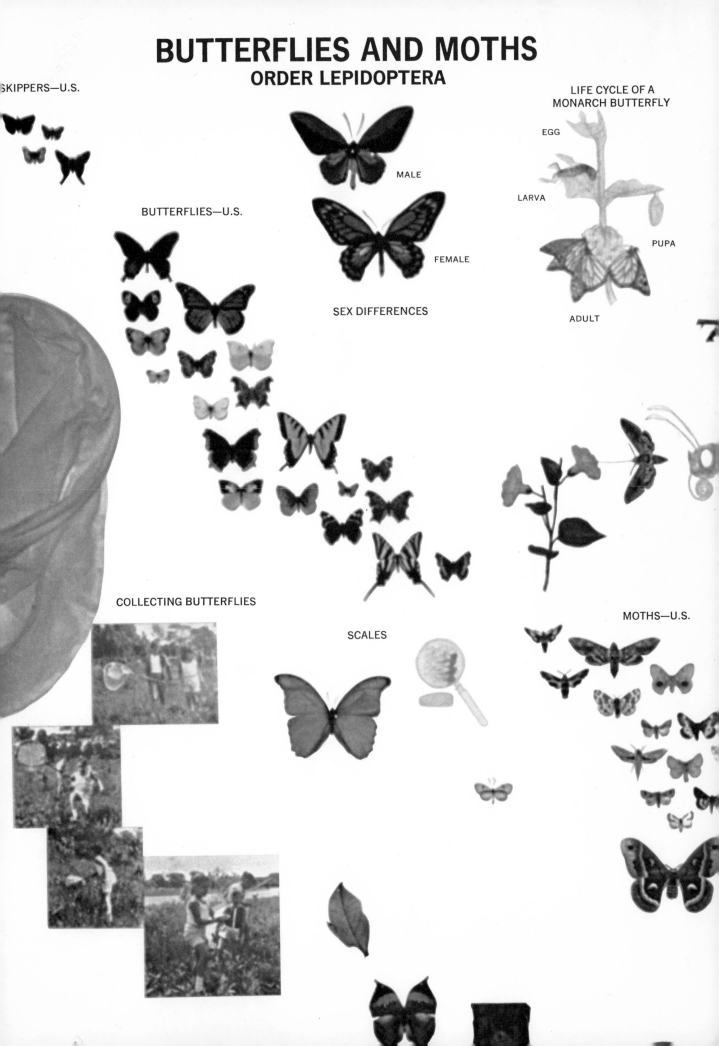

SKIPPERS—U.S.

BUTTERFLIES—U.S.

MALE

FEMALE

SEX DIFFERENCES

LIFE CYCLE OF A
MONARCH BUTTERFLY

EGG

LARVA

PUPA

ADULT

COLLECTING BUTTERFLIES

SCALES

MOTHS—U.S.

Butterflies are divided in two groups: true butterflies, the Papilionsidea, and the Hesperidii family, or Skippers. They are so much alike that they are usually referred to under the term "butterflies." However, they do have a number of characteristic differences that separate them. But butterflies and moths, even though they are linked together so closely in people's minds, are really quite different from each other. Although there is no single part or characteristic that can be used to distinguish *all* butterflies from *all* moths, here are some of the differences between the two.

1. Butterflies fly by day. They are usually inactive on cloudy days. Most moths fly at night, although quite a few are also day flyers.

2. Butterflies usually rest with their wings held upright over their backs. Moths, on the other hand, usually rest with their wings flat against their sides or flat over their backs. But there are exceptions in both groups.

3. Butterflies have a clublike swelling at or near the tip of each antenna, sometimes gradual and not noticeable, sometimes large and noticeable. The antennae of moths are usually hairlike and tapering, although in some families they may be comblike or feathery. But a few moths have antennae that end in the true butterfly clublike swelling.

4. Butterflies lock their fore-and hind wings together during flight by pressing the expanded front edge of the hind wing against the rear edge of the front wing. Most moths lock the two wings together by means of a strong bristle or group of bristles — the frenulum — found near the base of the front edge of the hind wing. But a few families of moths lack the frenulum or bristles.

5. The scales of butterflies are usually smaller, or more numerous, and more firmly attached to the wings than those of the moths.

BUTTERFLY

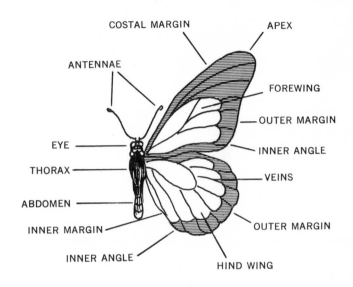

COSTAL MARGIN
APEX
ANTENNAE
FOREWING
OUTER MARGIN
INNER ANGLE
EYE
THORAX
VEINS
ABDOMEN
INNER MARGIN
OUTER MARGIN
INNER ANGLE
HIND WING

MOTH

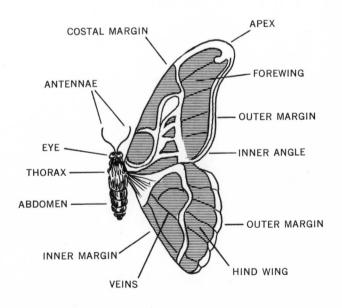

COSTAL MARGIN
APEX
ANTENNAE
FOREWING
OUTER MARGIN
INNER ANGLE
EYE
THORAX
ABDOMEN
OUTER MARGIN
INNER MARGIN
HIND WING
VEINS

BEGINNING OF A BUTTERFLY

All caterpillars develop into butterflies in the same way. We will see how a Monarch butterfly caterpillar changes. First it is a tiny egg which grows into a caterpillar. After a few weeks the caterpillar changes into a pupa, which is the third stage of butterfly development. From this pupa, the familiar adult Monarch butterfly emerges.

This Monarch caterpillar is feeding on its natural food plant, one of the milkweeds. The egg from which the caterpillar hatched was placed in another milkweed plant by its mother. This was not by chance. The mother picked the milkweed because it was the food upon which she herself was raised.

A typical caterpillar is made up of three body parts or regions. The *head* holds the chewing mouthparts and six, tiny, simple eyes on each side. The three-segmented (parted) *thorax* bears three pairs of true, jointed legs. The *abdomen* is made up of eleven segments. On its third, fourth, fifth, sixth, and eleventh segments, the caterpillar has pairs of fleshy prolegs that end in small, sharp hooks. Some caterpillars live in special ways and do not show all these parts and divisions clearly.

The bright colors of the Monarch caterpillar serve to warn birds and other enemies that it is not good to eat. Unless a young enemy, which does not know the Monarch butterfly tastes bad, attacks it, it has a good chance of growing safely to adulthood.

CATERPILLAR CHANGES TO A PUPA

The Monarch caterpillar eats and eats. It molts or sheds its skin several times, becoming fully grown in two or three weeks. It then stops eating and crawls into some safe place. There it can change into a pupa. On a twig or leaf from which it can hang, the caterpillar spins a firmly attached thin layer of silk over the supporting surface. It holds onto this pad of silk with its last prolegs and swings free, hanging its head downward.

The rate of pupa development is partially due to the temperature. The higher the temperature the faster the rate of development. While it hangs upside down, its skin loosens, as the pupa finishes developing within. Then the caterpillar's skin splits behind its head and is rolled upward. This reveals the pupa which is like a sleeping bag. When the skin is rolled all the way up, the hold of the proleg is loosened. Now a fine-hooked spike at the rear end of the pupa, the cremaster, must catch the silk pad. If it should miss, the pupa would fall. The pupa hangs head downward, supported by the cremaster and the silk pad. The caterpillar is no more. The change from caterpillar to mature pupa takes about twenty-four hours.

FULLY FORMED PUPA

The freshly formed Monarch pupa, or "chrysalis," is a very beautiful sight. In its earlier pupal stages, it is a pale, jade green color with gold markings. At a later stage the color changes to brown. Within a very short time after this color change occurs, the bright orange wings of the Monarch with their characteristic black markings, can be seen through the transparent skin of the pupa. On its surface can be traced the outlines of the eyes, antennae, mouthparts, and legs of the adult butterfly. Although the pupa hangs quietly, there is great activity within as the body parts of the caterpillar are remade into those of the butterfly. Even slight damage to the pupa may be very serious, preventing proper development of the encased butterfly.

The pupal stage of the Monarch lasts from ten days to two weeks. However, temperature plays an important part. Some butterflies may spend only seven or eight days as pupae; but others, especially in colder regions, may pass the winter in this stage. Pupae do not eat during this period of development and need only very small amounts of oxygen to survive.

MONARCH READY TO LEAVE PUPA

Finally the adult butterfly is ready to emerge from its isolation. Its colors and the pattern of its wings in perfect miniature, can be seen through the transparent pupal shell. The body fluids are pumped into the head and thorax with enough force to crack open the shell. Through this opening the head and the thorax push out, the legs are withdrawn, and the abdomen is pulled clear. The butterfly then moves. It must hang with its back down in order to expand its wings.

Butterflies usually come out of the pupal stage during the day when sunlight is present. The Monarch is a helpless creature when it first emerges. Its wings are soft and of no use at that time. Because of this, the young butterfly can be easily captured by one of its enemies. Therefore, it is important that the wings dry out quickly in the sun.

It is at this point that the "red rain" phenomenon may occur. Shortly after leaving the pupal stage, the adult butterfly secretes a drop or two of liquid. These drops are called meconium, which is made up of nitrogen wastes that have gathered in its body during the pupal stage. They are often red or pink in color. When meconium is spattered over leaves and fences, as it may be when large numbers of butterflies emerge in one locality, the effect suggests red rain.

ADULT MONARCH BUTTERFLY

The newly emerged butterfly must swallow sufficient air to fill its crop, which is a large pocket in the butterfly's digestive tract. It also must suck enough air through the breathing holes (spiracles) along each side of its body to fill its lungs. The pressure of the air thus built up, as well as the pressure produced by muscular contractions, forces blood into the wings. The wings slowly expand; their membranes come together, fuse, and stiffen. Then the blood is drawn back into the body; and the stiffened, drying wings remain expanded.

The two halves of the long "tongue," or proboscis, slender and flexible as they are, must be fitted and locked together, and the resulting slender tube is coiled in place beneath the head.

In a period of fifteen minutes to an hour, the butterfly will be ready to begin its new aerial life and to fulfill its reason for existence: the reproduction of its own kind.

Courtesy of CCM: General Biological Inc., Chicago

OUTSTANDING FAMILIES OF BUTTERFLIES

FAMILY	DISTRIBUTION	CHARACTERISTICS
HESPERIDAE Skippers	Worldwide	Body large and stout. Wings small and pointed. Antennae with club subapical and apex hooked. Front legs of both sexes normal.
PAPILIONIDAE Swallowtails	Worldwide	Some species are large. Hind wings often tailed. Front legs of both sexes normal.
PIERIDAE Whites and Sulphurs	Worldwide	Mostly white, yellow or orange. Front legs of both sexes normal.
LYCAENIDAE Blues, Coppers & Hairstreaks	Worldwide	Small. Front legs of males considerably reduced, of females only slightly reduced. The Blues are more whitish than blue and are smaller than the others. The Hairstreaks often have fine tails on the hind wings, though many species in the tropics lack them.
RIODINIDAE Metalmarks	Worldwide	Bewildering combinations of colors and wing shapes. Small. Front legs of males slightly reduced, of females normal.
MORPHOIDAE Morphoes	New World Tropics only	Most species are large. Brilliant, scintillating blue wings often used in objects of art. Front legs of both sexes reduced.
BRASSOLIDAE Owl Butterflies	Tropics only	Large. Some with wing expanse of over 5 inches. Undersurface of hind wings has eyelike spot. Hind wings often larger than fore wings. Front legs of both sexes reduced.
NYMPHALIDAE Brush-footed Butterflies	Worldwide	Front legs reduced to small brushlike eye-cleaner.
HELICONIIDAE & ITHOMIIDAE Mimics & Models	New World Tropics	Conspicuously patterned. Most species very distasteful. Bodies tough and rubbery. Front legs greatly reduced.
SATYRIDAE Wood Nymphs & Satyrs	Worldwide	Medium in size. Usually dull brown. Underside of each wing usually has one or more ringed eye-spots. Bases of front wing veins swollen. Front legs greatly reduced.
DANAIDAE Milkweed Butterflies & Monarchs	Worldwide	Tough, rubbery bodies. Wings conspicuously patterned. Front legs greatly reduced.

HABITS	LARVAE	PUPAE
Flight swift and darting. Flower visitors.	Plain and dull in color. Have a distinct "neck."	Often in a loosely woven silk cocoon.
Flight powerful, often soaring high. Flower visitors.	Brightly colored and patterned. Have protective scent organs, called osmeteria.	Hung by girdle and cremaster. Pupa with frontal horn on head.
Flight strong and vigorous. Flower visitors.		Hung by girdle and cremaster.
Tend to move hind wings when at rest.	Stout and sluglike. Many secrete honeydew relished by ants. Often live in ant nests.	Stout, oval. Hung by girdle and cremaster.
Flight fast, erratic and near ground.	Stout and sluglike, but often long-haired.	
Flight strong. Often soar in forest canopy.	Social. Have many poisonous hairs.	Pupate communally in a jointly spun web.
Flight strong.		
Flight strong. Flower visitors.	Usually spiny or with spiny tubercles.	Often very spiny and brightly colored.
Fly boldly and slowly out in the open.	Slender, spiny and irregularly shaped.	Irregularly shaped, with tubercles.
Flight jerky and fluttering. Fly low and seek cover when alarmed.	Spindle-shaped. Usually plain and inconspicuously colored. Last abdominal segment forked.	Sometimes in a silk-lined cell in detritus on ground.
Fly boldly far from shelter.	Boldly patterned. Often with bright stripes or spots. Two pairs of long filaments. Distasteful. Feed on milkweeds.	Stout. Suspended by cremaster only.

AFRICAN SKIPPERS

There are many families of butterflies found throughout the world from the steamy, hot jungles to the snowy, cold mountains. However, we are only going to learn about the butterflies found most frequently in a tropical climate.

The most primitive of all butterflies are the Skippers. They are found worldwide, but the tropical Skippers tend to be larger and more brilliantly colored than those found in more temperate regions.

This species of *Abantis* and some very similar close relatives are found in many parts of Africa. They are appropriately called African Skippers. The pair shown here come from the Congo. African Skippers have hooked tips on their antennae and relatively large heads and bodies. Both features are characteristic of Skippers.

The conspicuous white spots on the wings are bright and distinct in African Skippers. However, as some of the scales are rubbed off the wings, as they will be when the butterflies have been flying for awhile, the white spots will appear yellowish. Remember the beautiful colors of a butterfly's wing are not in the wing membrane itself. The colors are in the scales which lie overlapping, shingle-like, upon all butterflies' wings.

LARGE SOUTH AMERICAN SKIPPER

The New World, from Mexico to southern Argentina, is the home of a relatively enormous number of Skippers. There are many exceedingly large and attractive species in other tropical regions, such as the African Zambesian Skipper, but a collection from Central and South America invariably outshines those of other regions.

This large butterfly, photographed alive in Peru, belongs to the genus *Jemadia*. It has an intricate pattern of black, iridescent blue, and white that seems very distinctive. However, it has dozens of relatives, some close and some rather distant, that have much the same appearance. Other members of this family have long, graceful tails on the hind wings. Still others combine black with crimson, or orange, or deep, sapphire blue. This spectacular display of colors rivals any but the most outstanding butterflies.

The very large, streamlined body of a Skipper is packed with powerful flight muscles. These, combined with relatively short wings, enable it to fly erratically and exceedingly fast. Frequently a big Skipper will suddenly appear on a flower you are admiring — and then, just as suddenly, it is gone. Perhaps it appears again forty feet away, darting down to another flower or having aerial combat with another Skipper.

IMPERIAL SWALLOWTAIL

Throughout the world, there are many species of Swallowtails belonging to the great genus *Papilio*. Most of them are large and brightly colored. They often have graceful tails on their hind wings.

The shape of the forewings and the notched, tailed hind wings proclaim this to be a Swallowtail, but a most unusual one in a separate genus all by itself. The distinctive color pattern tells us that it is *Teinopalpus imperialis*, the Hope or Imperial Swallowtail. This is found only in India and central China at elevations of six to ten thousand feet. It may live in wooded districts, but is most commonly found on the very tops of mountains where there are open places. The Imperial Swallowtail has a wing expanse of well over three inches. It is an exceedingly fast flier and usually remains in or around the treetops, only rarely flying lower. The best way to catch it, therefore, is to put out baits of rotting fruits or dead animals.

The lovely glowing-green colors of the Imperial Swallowtail have a considerable camouflage value. They conceal the butterfly when it is resting among green leaves or when the female is crawling over foliage to lay her eggs.

SOUTH AMERICAN SWALLOWTAILS

Another group of Swallowtails is found only in the New World. They are called Fluted Swallowtails, because they have a graceful fluted fold along the anal margin of each hind wing. Many of the North American Swallowtails belong to this group, but in the tropics there are many more.

These large Swallowtails were photographed in Peru, where they were drinking at the edge of a shallow mud puddle. This is a very common habit among many groups of butterflies. Collectors often see masses ranging from dozens to hundreds of individuals tightly packed together, refreshing themselves.

A close relative of this species extends as far north as Connecticut. Its big brown-and-white caterpillars, which are called "orange dogs," may become abundant enough to be serious pests in orange and other citrus fruit orchards. They may even defoliate the trees. But, for the most part, the caterpillars of Fluted Swallowtails are not injurious to man's interests.

AFRICAN SWALLOWTAIL

This big Swallowtail, *Papilio demodocus* Linnaeus, which ranges widely in tropical Africa, was photographed in the Belgian Congo, sunning itself in an open area. It is one of the many species of Swallowtails, some of which are found in tropical regions all over the world, that do not have tails on the hind wings. At first glance we might not think it a close relative of the graceful, long-tailed "true" Swallowtails. But all of its structures, such as the arrangement of wing veins and the front legs, as well as the peculiar scent organs which it has as a caterpillar, identify it as a Swallowtail. The presence or absence of tails is of no great importance in its classification. There are in Africa, as a matter of fact, some Swallowtails in which most of the males have tails, but only some of the females have them. This lack of tails may even be a matter of variation from one region to another, or of mimicry of other butterflies.

WHITE KITE SWALLOWTAIL

Still another group of Swallowtails are the Kite Swallowtails, now put in the genus *Graphium*, although formerly in the genus *Papilio*. They are recognized by their thinly scaled, usually brightly colored wings and by their long pointed tails. Only a few species are found in temperate regions, but there are dozens in the tropics.

Kite Swallowtails are found in sunny clearings from Mexico to Brazil and Bolivia. They are speedy and agile fliers and very clever at escaping the net. The females tend to stay in the woods, but the males can often be seen gathered in large numbers at mud puddles and other moist places. When drinking, they rest with a characteristic quivering motion of half-open wings.

This gathering of large swarms of young bachelor males to suck moisture is characteristic not only of the Kite Swallowtails but of other Swallowtails, Sulphurs, and other butterflies. Sometimes such swarms at mud puddles will be made up of so many hundreds of butterflies that it can be seen from a great distance.

UPPER SIDE, DELIAS WHITES

The large genus *Delias* is one of the characteristic groups of Whites in the Indo-Australian region. Once this species was considered quite rare. However, within the last fifty years a few adventurous explorers have gone to the great highlands of interior New Guinea, discovering dozens of new species. There are still probably many unknown ones awaiting further exploration and discovery.

The majority of *Delias* are plain white on the upper side, with dark borders, but on the underside are extraordinarily and brilliantly colored and patterned. Each new species provides a new and unexpected combination of colors. This photograph shows the upper sides of two *Delias* Whites. The smaller butterfly is *Delias leucias* Jordan species. It has a wingspread of one and three-quarters inches. The larger specimen is *Delias gabia zerate* Smith, with a wing expanse of two inches.

UNDERSIDE, DELIAS WHITES

Here are the very different undersides of the two *Delias* Whites. Now we get an idea of the surprise that one always encounters in turning over a specimen of *Delias*.

Most of the known species of *Delias* are found in grassy country and open woodlands at moderate elevations of 2500 to 8000 feet. They fly during the early hours of the day around the treetops. Occasionally they glide over a grassy plain in a lazy, irregular flight, staying close to the ground to visit flowers. The females seldom come down from the treetops until late afternoon. The female *Delias* Whites are brightly colored. They fly openly and use their bold colors and patterns to warn possible enemies that either their odor or taste would make them distasteful meals.

One species has been observed migrating from one valley to another, going forth in the evening and returning to the same locality the next morning.

AVELLANADA'S GIANT SULPHUR

Phoebis avellanada Herrich-Schaeffer is the largest and most brilliantly colored member of its genus. It has a wing expanse of well over three inches. The genus includes most of the Giant Sulphurs of the New World and is found mainly in the tropics. The similar-looking Giant Sulphurs of the Old World tropics are in the genus *Catopsilia*. They also are large butterflies with bold colors of white, yellow, and orange. Along with the Kite Swallowtails, Sulphurs are among the most consistent mud-puddle visitors. Groups of several hundred may often be seen drinking together.

Giant Sulphurs are best known for their migratory habits. Swarms, numbering millions, may often be seen flying along the banks of a river, pouring across a mountain pass, or even flying hundreds of miles out to sea where eventually all must perish. These are not true migrations with a return flight. They are one-way flights which may result in the settlement of many new areas.

PURPLE-TIPPED WHITE

This extremely beautiful butterfly was photographed in the Congo. It is a member of the large genus *Teracolus* of the family of the Whites and Sulphurs (Pieridae). The great majority of the species of this genus are African, although some are found in the Near East and southern Asia. Most of them are white, but some are yellow or salmon-yellow. Their most distinctive feature is the very bright colors found on the top portion of each front wing. In most of the species this is yellow or orange, in some it is scarlet or, as in the species shown here, a scarlet overlaid with iridescent purple or violet.

Some Orange-Tipped Whites gather in very large numbers, and one or two types have been recorded as damaging cultivated crops. But this is rare. When they swarm, they may fly for considerable distances straight across country, giving the appearance of a mass migration.

TROPICAL EUMAEUS

Butterflies of the family Lycaenidae are often called the "Children of the Sun," because of the way they playfully flit around the tops of trees and shrubs or wander along the roadside when the sun shines brightly. But as soon as the sun clouds over, they slip away into the shrubbery where they rest, hidden beneath the leaves or leaf stalks.

Of the three groups of Lycaenids only the Coppers are not common in the tropics. The Blues and Hairstreaks are found in great numbers both in the tropics and in temperate regions.

This little *Eumaeus minijas* Huebner has a wing expanse of two inches. It is larger than most of the Blues and has a deeper, brighter blue color. But despite these differences, it is much like its relatives in habits and behavior.

One similar species, *Eumaeus atala* from Cuba and Florida, has been almost exterminated in the Florida Everglades where it formerly was abundant. However, there are signs that it may be slowly coming back in small numbers. It is hoped that with proper protection in the Everglades National Park the sole North American representative of this interesting tropical butterfly will again become populous.

SOUTH AMERICAN HAIRSTREAK

The Hairstreaks are one of the great worldwide divisions of the Lycaenidae. Most of them are small. They are named for the hairlike tails found on their hind wings and the streaky markings on their wings. Many Hairstreaks are among the most beautiful of all butterflies despite their small size. It is almost impossible to guess from the appearance of the upper side of the wing what the underside of the wing will look like. One group of species, like this *aetolus* specimen, will be boldly striped. Those of another group, looking very similar above, will be deep brown with red spots, or pearly gray crisscrossed with blue lines.

The caterpillars of many Hairstreaks, as well as of Blues and Coppers, lead lives of great cooperation with ants. The caterpillars have a honey gland which secretes a sweet honeydew that is eaten by ants. In return for this food, the ants may act as guards for the caterpillars on their food plants. They may even take them to live in their nest. Here the caterpillars may feed on the ants' brood for awhile and then change into the pupa stage of life. When the adult Hairstreak leaves its pupa, it rushes out of the the ant nest, spreads its wings, and flies away.

LARGE SOUTH AMERICAN HAIRSTREAK

The large South American Hairstreak is not an uncommon butterfly. It is frequently found in open glades. However, it is extremely difficult to capture a perfect specimen because the long tails on the hind wings are very fragile. These tails are merely extensions of the delicate wing membrane, not supported or strengthened in any way by veins. As a result, they break off very easily even when the South American Hairstreak is flying normally about its affairs. When a specimen is caught in a net and struggles to escape, some or even all of its tails are almost sure to be lost. As is so often the case, the only way to be sure of getting perfect specimens is to raise them from eggs or caterpillars. However, this has been done for so comparatively few of the tropical species that one hardly knows how to begin.

The long tails of the Hairstreak are believed to have a protective value. Birds or lizards often mistake the very prominent rear end of the Hairstreak for its front end with its long antennea, and grab it instead of the vulnerable head. An attack on its rear does the butterfly little harm. It can fly quite well minus most of its hind wings. Thus it survives many enemy attacks.

SOUTH AMERICAN METALMARK

The Metalmarks of the family Erycinidae are a worldwide family with some representatives in every great faunal region. But in South America there are ten times as many as in all the rest of the world combined. The South American species show an unbelievable number of different colors, patterns, and wing shapes. Some are as brilliantly iridescent blue as any of the Hairstreaks or the big Morphoes. Others are extremely plain, checkered-brown and difficult to see among dead foliage. Still others have long tails on the hind wings, like the Hairstreak. Some Metalmarks are black with orange bands, copying the markings of the bad tasting moths. Others have developed black transparent wings, and are almost perfect mimics of some of the highly protected, foul tasting Ithomiid butterflies.

This Metalmark is a member of the genus *Amarynthus*. It is one of the brightly colored species that is extremely conspicuous when flying in the sunshine. However, the brilliant colors, combined with a fast wingbeat and erratic flight, actually have an almost dazzling effect. It is not nearly as easy to catch this outstanding Metalmark in flight as one might think.

SOUTH AMERICAN METALMARK

In comparison with the other South American Metalmark with its brilliant colors and bold patterns, this specimen is relatively modest in appearance. It shows traces of the checkered brown-and-white pattern characteristic of many members of the family from other parts of the world. But the big eyespots on the front wings are characteristic of those found in Central and South America. Some of its close relatives have the same kind of eyespots, but their wings are bright blue and black.

Eyespots are another way butterflies protect themselves. Their sudden exposure, when the butterfly alights on a leaf and opens its wings out flat (a characteristic Metalmark position), has been shown to have a startling effect on birds, delaying their pecking reaction, often giving the Metalmark just enough time to escape.

GIANT BLUE MORPHO

Once seen, the colors of the Morpho are unforgettable. For the most part the colors are not due to the presence of chemicals or pigments. They are the result of the effect light has when it strikes tiny structures deep within the Morpho's wing scales. These small structures beneath the scales break up and bend the light rays in such a way that only blue and red can be seen. The blue of the Morpho wing, as well as nearly all the blues of other insects, most greens, and certainly all iridescence, are due to similar light breaking structures. These brilliant body colors cannot be dissolved or faded. They can disappear temporarily, however, when a wing is wet. The colors can be altered when the angle of light striking the light breaking structures changes. The structures which cause these colors are of several different types. One of them has been named the Morpho type because it is so strikingly presented in butterflies of this genus.

The Morpho is found in the western hemisphere from central Mexico to southern Brazil. This species, *Morpho rhetenor* Cramer, has a wing expanse of nearly five inches.

OWL BUTTERFLY

Owl butterflies have a wing expanse of as much as five and one-half inches. This individual was photographed resting on an orchid in Colombia. It lives exclusively in the dense forests of the New World tropics, and flies only in shady places or on dark days. It hides in the thickets, landing near the base of tree trunks with wings outspread. It is attracted to the liquid that comes out of damaged trees, and may be baited with fermenting fruit.

Owl butterflies are noted for the large, eyelike markings on the underside of each hind wing. This picture shows not only the markings but also the velvety texture of the underside of the wings. The upper side of the wing (not visible here) is a solid, rich brown with a purple sheen. A single broad band of yellow runs across each hind wing.

People have seen a striking resemblance to an owl's face in the markings on the underside of the Owl butterfly's hind wings. It has been assumed that the purpose of this owl-like appearance is to frighten enemies. However, this is not a proven fact. Still, the sudden exposure of these spots may be enough to slow an attacker, giving the Owl butterfly enough time to escape capture and death.

CALICO BUTTERFLY

The clicking butterflies, or Calicoes, are common in Central America and Brazil. Their wing expanse is about two and one-half inches. They can be found in the sun, on walls or tree trunks, resting head down, wings outspread. Although they make frequent short flights, they usually return to the same resting place.

This group of butterflies *(Hamadryas* or *Ageronia)* is of historical interest because it was observed by Charles Darwin when he made the famous trip related in *The Voyage of H.M.S. Beagle*. His well-known description is of special interest to us:

> *" . . . But a far more singular fact is the power which this species possesses of making a noise. Several times when a pair, probably male and female, were chasing each other in an irregular course, they passed within a few yards of me; and I distinctly heard a clicking noise, similar to that produced by a toothed wheel passing under a spring catch. The noise was continued at short intervals, and could be distinguished at about twenty yards' distance . . . "

Since then many collectors have heard this same noise. It is believed to be made by structures located at the base of the Calico's forewings.

*Darwin, Charles. *Natural History and Geology of the Countries Visited during the Voyage Round the World of the H.M.S. 'Beagle'*. New York: D. Appleton & Co., 1890.

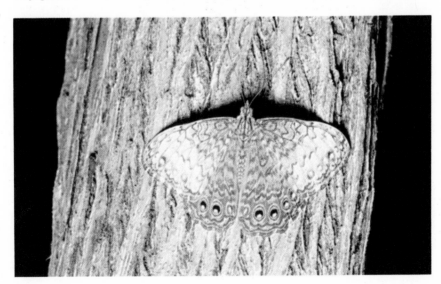

SOUTH AMERICAN "88" BUTTERFLY

Strictly speaking, this is not a true "88" butterfly, for on the underside of each hind wing there should be two double spots, forming a pair of eights. In this species one of the spots is single. However, it is one of a group of closely related nymphalid genera, *Callicore*, *Diaethria*, *Catagramma*, and a few others, that show this characteristic type of marking. All are small- to medium-sized, and most have iridescent blue or scarlet bands on the upper sides of their wings. Some of the species are rare, but many are very common. They are frequently caught because hundreds of them habitually gather to drink from wet mud along the banks of streams and ponds. As a result, they are well-represented in every collection of New World tropical butterflies.

These butterflies have a curious and characteristic structural feature — the bases of some of the front wing veins are considerably swollen and hollow. It is possible that these act as a vibrating chamber for a hearing organ.

SOUTH AMERICAN AGRIAS BUTTERFLY

Long prized because of their brilliance and beauty, specimens of this genus were once believed to be very rare. Museums and owners of private collections paid fantastic prices for a South American *Agrias* butterfly.

However, now more is known about their habits, and they are being caught with increasing frequency. If one knows where to look for them and how to collect them, they can be found. They seldom gather or fly in large numbers. They are more likely to be found flying alone. Though fast fliers, they are timid in flight. Having selected a resting place they tend to sit for some time. If disturbed they fly away, but they return to the same spot as soon as possible.

One collector writes vividly of seeing one come to rest high on a jungle tree. However he had nothing long enough to reach it. Hastily he cut down a young sapling, trimmed off its branches, and fastened a net bag to its end. But it was not long enough so he made a longer one. This homemade net handle was so long and slender that it swayed almost uncontrollably as the collector stretched toward the resting butterfly. Still the *Agrias* did not move, and the collector captured it.

Agrias claudia lugens Fruhstorfer, the specimen seen here, has a wing expanse of over three inches.

SOUTH AMERICAN SCARLET STRIPE

This butterfly, *Anartia amathea* Linnaeus, was photographed visiting flowers in Colombia, South America. One of the most widespread butterflies of the New World tropics, the Scarlet Stripe ranges from Mexico southward through most of tropical South America. It is found nearly everywhere. Sometimes it is so abundant that it is one of the butterflies almost certain to be captured in the tropics and to be represented in every collection. It is, moreover, quite easy to catch, although it can fly swiftly when alarmed. The Scarlet Stripe is greatly addicted to visiting flowers, particularly those of weeds growing along roads and in open places. And knowing this habit, the collector can often ambush one.

The Scarlet Stripe's appearance has considerable geographic variation. Series of specimens from different regions show a good deal of difference in the width and extent of the red stripe across the wings. The size of the white- or cream-colored spots also varies. Some of the geographic differences are so distinct that they have been further classified and given special names.

AFRICAN CHARAXES

The butterflies of this genus *Charaxes* are as characteristic of Africa as lions and zebras. A great number of species are only found there, many being especially typical of the great equatorial forests of the Congo. These butterflies are medium-sized to large, with wingspreads up to three inches. Some are strong, high fliers. Many have two, short, sharp tails on each hind wing, like the species of the *jasius* group shown in this photograph. The bold, detailed underside patterns are not repeated on the upper sides, which generally are plainly colored or dully iridescent.

The fact that this *Charaxes* was photographed in a swarm of other butterflies sipping liquid is very typical. *Charaxes* will be attracted by such wet baits as rotten fruits. Thus, they can be caught in large numbers.

INDIAN LEAF BUTTERFLY

The dead-leaf butterflies are often said to be the most remarkable examples of protective coloration found in nature. In the New World, butterflies of the genus *Anaea* are well known for their dead-leaf appearance. However, in the Old World it is the genus *Kallima* that is outstanding. This species, *Kallima inachus* Boisduval, is widespread in India and China. It has a wing expanse of over two and one-half inches.

In 1869, Alfred Russel Wallace, the famous naturalist who simultaneously propounded with Darwin the principles of natural selection which so changed and influenced all biological thought, described the *Kallima* butterflies in his book *The Malay Archipelago*. He had repeatedly caught a glimpse of them, but whenever he attempted to capture one it would vanish into a bush among dry or dead leaves. Search as he might, he could never find one after it had thus disappeared, until it once again took to the air. Upon examining a captured specimen of *Kallima paralekta*, he wrote:

> *"The end of the upper wing terminates in a fine point, just as the leaves of many tropical shrubs and trees are pointed . . . The tint of the under surface varies much but it is always some ashy brown or reddish color, which matches with those of dead leaves. The habit of the species is always to rest on a twig and among dry or dead leaves, and in this position with the wings closely pressed together, their outline is exactly that of a moderately-sized leaf, slightly curved or shrivelled. The tail of the hind wings forms a perfect stalk, and touches the stick while the insect is supported by the middle pair of legs, which are not noticed among the twigs and fibers that surround it."

*Wallace, Alfred Russel. *The Malay Archipelago*. London: MacMillan & Co., 1869.

UPPER SIDE

UNDERSIDE

MOTHONE AND BICOLORED MIMIC

Melinaea mothone Hewitson, shown at the top of this photograph, is a butterfly of the family Ithomiidae. *Heliconius aristiona bicolorata* Butler, shown below it, is a member of the family Heliconiidae. They each have a wing expanse of about three and one-quarter inches. Each one is boldly patterned and colored. This warns their enemies that they are distasteful and are to be left alone. The two are so similar in appearance that it is difficult to tell them apart. However, a bird, or other enemy, does not need to tell them apart. The enemy needs only to learn from one bad experience this one warning pattern. Having done this, he will avoid any creature of the same general shape and coloration. Because of this simple learning process, the two species shown here have an increased chance of survival. This type of mimicry or copying between two unrelated forms, each distasteful in itself, is called Müllerian mimicry.

CLEAR-WING ITHOMIID BUTTERFLY

One of the most characteristic groups of the New World tropical butterflies is the family Ithomiidae. Scores of species are found throughout Central and South America. These are highly protected butterflies — that is, they have strong body secretions that make them distasteful to such enemies as birds and lizards. Like their near relatives, the Heliconiids, they give warning of their bad taste with characteristic, bright color patterns. Their largely transparent wings (which actually conceal them at times) with an eye-catching band of yellow or white across each front wing, make it easier for enemies to learn to recognize and avoid them.

Many other butterflies and moths mimic these Ithomiids. Some of them (Heliconiids and other Ithomiids, and certain *Dismorphia* Pierids) are also bad tasting. Therefore, their copying of the Ithomiids' characteristics is another example of Müllerian mimicry. But many others, such as some of the Metalmarks and moths of several families, are probably not genuinely foul tasting themselves. But by evolving the appearance of the Ithomiids, they share in their protection. This type of mimicry is called Batesian mimicry after the distinguished English naturalist Henry Bates, who first identified it.

TRANSPARENT-WING BUTTERFLY

Collecting butterflies in tropical forests is an exciting and at times a strange experience. It is an adventure that is always rich in surprises and full of unforgettably beautiful sights. The giant Morphoes float high overhead, flashing their brilliant blues and then apparently vanishing from sight as the dull undersides of their wings are exposed by the tilting of the wings. The bright jewel-like wings of numerous vividly colored *Agrias* wink from the treetops, and large, richly colored Owl butterflies slowly alight on a tree trunk. One of the most beautiful sights a collector can have comes when the rosy-tipped Transparent-Wing butterfly comes from the shadows. At times only its pink tips can be seen against the forest background. But when it moves into a shaft of light, the entire wing membrane reflects the light like a mirror. Then—it is gone.

Cithaerias pireta Cramer, from the upper Amazon basin, has a wing expanse of two inches. Despite its delicate appearance, it is a Satyrid, related to the hardy looking, dull-brown Wood Nymphs found in temperate regions.

A GLOSSARY OF TERMS

antenna   —one of the paired, movable, jointed appendages on the head of an insect.

apex   —pointed or angular end, highest point.

apical   —belonging to the apex or top.

chrysalis   —the inactive form, or pupa, of an insect, from which the active form emerges.

cocoon   —the envelope spun by certain larval insects.

cremaster   —the stout spine at the anal end of a pupa.

cryptic   —form or color that serves for concealment.

detritus   —rubbish, loose particles, waste.

exudate   —discharged liquid, gum or moisture, as from a plant.

filament   —a threadlike structure.

frenulum   —a spine on the hind wing of certain Lepidoptera, which acts as a hook to hold the two wings together in flight.

girdle   —a silk band that aids in supporting the chrysalis of some butterflies.

larva   —the stage of metamorphosis preceding the pupa, also called a caterpillar.

metamorphosis   —a passing from one stage or form into another.

osmeterium   —an organ for producing or emitting an odor.

predator   —a creature which lives by preying on others.

proboscis   —in the Lepidoptera, a tubular mouth structure used for feeding.

proleg   —one of the fleshy abdominal legs of many insect larvae.

pupa   —the third stage of an insect that undergoes a normal complete metamorphosis.

pupate   —to enter upon or undergo the pupal condition.

spiracle   —the external opening of the trachea of an insect (see *trachea*).

subapical   —below or near the apex.

thorax   —the region of the insect's body that bears legs and wings.

trachea   —an air tube or passage through which air is conveyed.

tubercle   —a small, knoblike growth.

venation   —the arrangement or disposition of veins.

BIBLIOGRAPHY

Here are some books about tropical butterflies to give
you more knowledge about this fascinating subject.

Butler, William. *The Butterfly Revolution*. New York:
    G.P. Putnam's Sons, 1967.

Conklin, Gladys. *I Like Butterflies*. New York: Holiday House, 1960.

Ehrlich, Paul R., and Anne H., ed. *How to Know the Butterflies*.
    Dubuque, Iowa: W.C. Brown Company, 1961.

Farb, Peter. *The Story of Butterflies and Other Insects*.
    Irvington-on-Hudson, New York: Harvey House, Inc., 1959.

Godwin, Elizabeth. *Child's Book of Butterflies*. Chicago:
    Maxton Company, 1956.

Hogner, Dorothy. *Butterflies*. New York: T.Y. Crowell
    Company, 1962.

Hopf, A.L. *Monarch Butterflies*. New York: T.Y. Crowell
    Company, 1965.

Holland, H.J. *The Butterfly Book*. Garden City, New York:
    Doubleday & Company, Inc., 1931.

Klots, Alexander Barrett. *The World of Butterflies and Moths*.
    New York: McGraw-Hill, Inc., 1958.

McClung, Robert. *Moths and Butterflies and How They Live*.
    New York: William Morrow & Company, Inc., 1966.

Portmann, Adolf. *The Beauty of Butterflies*. London: Oxford
    University Press, 1948.

Rumaker, Michael. *The Butterfly*. New York: Charles Scribner's
    Sons, 1962.

Simon, Hilda. *Wonders of the Butterfly World*. New York: Dodd,
    Mead & Company, 1963.

Vanden Eeckhoudt, Jean Pierre. *A Butterfly Is Born*. New York:
    Sterling Publishing Company, 1960.

INDEX

127413

DATE DUE

FEB 2 1 1990			
FACULTY FEB 1 4 19			
DEC 1 2 1997			
DEC 2 8 199			

J 595.78 K
Klots, Alexander Barrett,
 1903-
Tropical butterflies

Ohio Dominican College Library
1216 Sunbury Road
Columbus, Ohio 43219

DEMCO